LYRICS FOR A LUTE

Lyrics for a Lute

By

FRANK DEMPSTER SHERMAN

BOSTON AND NEW YORK
HOUGHTON, MIFFLIN AND COMPANY
The Riverside Press, Cambridge
MDCCCXCV

FOURTH EDITION.

The Riverside Press, Cambridge, Mass., U. S. A.
Electrotyped and Printed by H. O. Houghton & Co.

To
JULIET

CONTENTS.

FANCY

TO FANCY.

FROM what mystery of space
Come you, miracle of grace!
Lighting up the realm of dream
With a transitory gleam?
Phantom of the poet's brain!
From what shadowy domain
Come you secretly, unsought,
Making music of his thought,
Bringing him the gift of rhyme
At an unexpected time?
Is there any magic lure
That will win you quick and sure?
Is there any fetter strong
That will hold you, soul of song?
Tell me, Fancy, so that I
May not let you slip me by!

THE HARBOR OF DREAMS.

ONLY a whispering gale
  Flutters the wings of the boat;
Only a bird in the vale
  Lends to the silence a note
  Mellow, subdued, and remote:
This is the twilight of peace,
This is the hour of release,
Free of all worry and fret,
Clean of all care and regret,
When like a bird in its nest
Fancy lies folded to rest.

This is the margin of sleep;
  Here let the anchor be cast;
Here in forgetfulness deep,
  Now that the journey is past,
  Lower the sails from the mast.
Here is the bay of content,
Heaven and earth interblent;
Here is the haven that lies
Close to the gates of surprise;
Here all like Paradise seems,—
Here is the harbor of dreams.

BREATH OF SONG.

From the minster's organ-loft,
  Floating down the shadowed nave,
Comes a strain of music soft,
  Falling as a weary wave
    Falls upon the beach of sand,
    Murmurous and sweet and bland,
    Bearing from the mighty sea
    Messages of melody.

There, alone, the organist
  Lets his listless fingers go—
Lost in a melodious mist—
  O'er the key-board, to and fro:
    There, half-dreaming, in the gloom,
    Sits the weaver at his loom,
    Weaving with the threads of sound
    Music-woof the warp around.

All unconsciously he hides
  Strains familiar in his theme,
When a master-spirit glides
  Through the doorway of his dream;

Mozart, Handel, Chopin, or
Harmony's great conjuror —
Rapt Beethoven! — each is part
Of the dreaming player's heart.

So the Poet dreams, nor heeds
Who may listen, who may hear;
Following where Fancy leads,
She alone to him is dear:
Omar, Keats, Theocritus,
In his voice may speak to us
From the realm of ages dim —
These are in the heart of him!

Poets in the fields of Time,
Since the world began, have sown
Wide the precious seeds of rhyme,
And to us to-day are blown
Odors from these poem-flowers —
Seedlings of the later hours —
Blossoming the fields along,
Breathing the sweet breath of song.

OMAR KHAYYÁM.

At Naishápúr his ashes lie
  O'ershadowed by the mosque's blue
    dome;
There folded in his tent of sky
  The star of Persia sleeps at home.

The Rose her buried Nightingale
  Remembers, faithful all these years;
Around his grave the winds exhale
  The fragrant sorrow of her tears.

Sultans and slaves in caravans
  Since Malik Shah have gone their
    way,
And ridges in the Kubberstans
  Are their memorials to-day.

But from the dust in Omar's tomb
  A Fakir has revived a Rose,
Perchance the old, ancestral bloom
  Of that one by the mosque which
    blows;

And from its petals he has caught
  The inspiration Omar knew,
Who from the stars his wisdom brought, —
  A Persian Rose that drank the dew.

The Fakir now in dust lies low
  With Omar of the Orient;
Fitzgerald, shall we call him? No:
  'T was Omar in the Occident!

REVERY.

C. S.

GIVE me my happy poet's book
And let me find a sylvan nook,
Far from the noisy world apart,
And near enough to Nature's heart
To hear it throb and feel it thrill,
Yet wonder why 't is all so still:

There, thick with leaves, the branches spread
Their canopy of green o'erhead,
Through which in sudden wind-torn rifts
The sun its dusty copper sifts;
And there a dreamy brook runs by, —
A slender strip of twilight sky,
Starred with its ripples, and its moon
A lily lying in a swoon
Upon its bosom, wan and white
As that pale wanderer of night.

Birds in the arching boughs above
Fluting their melodies of love;
Bees in the distance humming where
The blossom's honey scents the air;
And, where the wild-flowers cluster, hosts
Of Psyches hovering like ghosts
Around the fragrant, curtained glooms,
Clouding the air with wingèd blooms.

There with my book, a flagon filled
With wine of song the poet spilled
From cups of love's sweet overflow
In happy riot, long ago, —
With Herrick, from whose well-tuned lute
First grew the lyric bud and fruit, —
There, in the shifting sun and shade,
In fancy I shall see that maid
To whom his songs, — each one of them
Clean cut and finished as a gem, —
He sang, until her every grace
Found in his limpid verse a place,
That she with him might live as long
As man is moved by love and song!

Oh, that we, too, who touch the string
To-day and set it quivering,

Whose hearts have caught one little
spark
Of rhyme in this prosaic dark,
Unto our verses might but give
That subtile touch to make them live,
Like Herrick's, after we are gone!
That all our lines might linger on
The lips of those who later shall
Love lyric brief and madrigal;
And immortality for us
In melody be vouchsafed thus!

AT MIDNIGHT.

SEE, yonder, the belfry tower
  That gleams in the moon's pale light;
Or is it a ghostly flower
  That dreams in the silent night?

I listen and hear the chime
  Go quavering o'er the town,
And out of this flower of Time
  Twelve petals are wafted down.

ISRAFEL.

FROM Paradise what soul with wings
In yonder green spray hides and sings,
Weaving within the fragrant gloom
Song-fabrics on the morning's loom?

'T is Israfel returned to us,
Making the world melodious:
He, he it is who sows the air
With seeds of music everywhere,
Until the charmèd space around
Grows sweet with blossomings of sound.

In ecstasy the fields lie mute,
Spelled by the magic of his lute;
The trees are hushed the while to hear
The cadence falling liquid-clear;
The winds hold in their breath, lest they
Cheat of one dulcet note the day;
And through the meadow, lisping low,
The naiads silver-sandaled go,
Or drowsy grown beside the streams,
Lie drinking music's wine of dreams;

And I, enraptured, in the dell
Pause, listening to Israfel:
Oblivious of all beside,
Dreaming, I drift upon the tide
Of melody until my eyes
Picture him there in Paradise, —
When lo, there comes a sudden hush;
'T is earth, — and yonder soars a thrush!

BACKLOG DREAMS.

ABOVE the glowing embers
  I hear the backlog sing
The music it remembers
  Of some remembered Spring;
Back to the branch forsaken
  Return its jocund choir
And in the chimney waken
  A melody of fire.

The sparks' red blossoms glisten
  And flash their glances brief
At me who lean and listen
  And dream I hear the leaf,
On some May morning sunny,
  Low lisping in the tree, —
Or, in his haunt of honey,
  A bloom-enamored bee:

Or 't is the soft wind blowing
  Its sweetness from the South,
A fragrant kiss bestowing
  Upon the rose's mouth;

And e'er the spell is broken,
  Or darkness o'er it slips,
I see the scarlet token
  Of love upon her lips.

Without, the storm is bitter,
  The snowflakes fill the night;
Within, the embers glitter
  And gild the room with light;
And in the fire-place gleaming
  The backlog sings away,
And mingles all my dreaming
  With birds and blooms and May.

SORCERY.

A ROSE on a spray where a brown bird sang,
Looked down, with a blush on her lovely face,
And saw, lying coiled in the fragrant place,
A green little snake with a forkèd fang.

Then swift from her cheek fled the crimson blush;
No longer she dreamed of the bird's sweet song;
But trembled with fear, lest the poisoned prong
Should strike and the lyric forever hush.

And lo, when the serpent had slipped away,
And vanished the bird in the blue above,

Two maids in the morning of new-found love
Bent over the bloom on the slender spray.

And one in her heart felt a strange delight, —
A thought of the bird made the rose blush red!
And one in her heart felt a sudden dread, —
A thought of the snake made the rose blanch white!

MOTHS.

Ghosts of departed wingèd things,
  What memories are those
That tempt you with your damask wings
  Here where my candle glows?

Vainly you hover, circling oft
  The tongue of yellow flame:
A tiger by caresses soft
  You vainly seek to tame.

Here is no hope for you: nay, here
  Death lurks within the light,
To leap upon you flying near
  And sweep you from the night.

Moon-butterflies, back to your blooms
  Born of the dew and stars!
Hence, ghosts, and find again your glooms
  Hidden by shadow-bars.

Quick, — speed across the dusky blue,
  Lest, in a sudden breath,
This tawny tiger wake, and you
  Endure a second death!

ON A GREEK VASE.

DIVINELY shapen cup, thy lip
  Unto me seemeth thus to speak:
"Behold in me the workmanship,
  The grace and cunning of a Greek!

"Long ages since he mixed the clay,
  Whose sense of symmetry was such,
The labor of a single day
  Immortal grew beneath his touch.

"For dreaming while his fingers went
  Around this slender neck of mine,
The form of her he loved was blent
  With every matchless curve and line.

"Her loveliness to me he gave
  Who gave unto herself his heart,
That love and beauty from the grave
  Might rise and live again in art."

And hearing from thy lips this tale
  Of love and skill, of art and grace,

Thou seem'st to me no more the frail
  Memento of an older race:

But in thy form divinely wrought
  And figured o'er with fret and scroll,
I dream, by happy chance was caught,
  And dwelleth now, that maiden's soul.

MOODS.

Upon a mountain-summit high,
A trysting-place of earth and sky,
Three friends once stood in silent awe,
Each contemplating what he saw.

One gazing on the landscape found
In changing features only sound:
To him it was a memory
Of some majestic symphony.

Another in the vastness caught
The essence of a poet's thought,
The measures of a noble rhyme
Enduring as eternal time.

The third — a stranger to those arts
That moved and thrilled his comrades'
hearts, —
Remembered with a nameless dread
The face of one whom he saw dead.

FULFILMENT.

In the hush of the night he heard
  A voice, and his heart said " Hark ! "
And the song of a distant bird
  Went quavering through the dark.

Like a lost little child it sobbed
  As far as the purple hill,
And the valley with music throbbed
  A moment, then all was still.

Then the heart in his bosom cried,
  " Alas, 't is a grievous wrong
That the multitude be denied
  The sweetness of such a song :

" 'T were a poet's divinest art
  The words of that song to write ! "
So he wrote for the eager heart
  The song of the bird at night.

And it went like the night-bird's voice
  Out into a world of gloom ;
And his heart had its dearest choice,
  And slept in a poet's tomb !

MNEMOSYNE'S MIRROR.

WHEN Summer comes and brings the rose,
My glass the winter's landscape shows:
The spectral wood and shrouded field,
The garden's lips in silence sealed,
The north-wind's icy bitter breath
As 't were the stirrup cup of death;
The pulseless brook, the absent song,
The sunlight brief and shadows long.

But comes December's day, and then
My mirror shows me June again:
The garden's million lips of bloom
Speaking their language of perfume;
The lyric quavers of the thrush
Shot, arrow like, across the hush;
The laughing brook, the lisping leaf,
The sunlight long and shadows brief.

Grant me, Mnemosyne, when old,
This magic mirror still to hold,

Transforming Time in such a way
That I shall see Youth's yesterday
Reflected there, and view once more
My boat upon Life's morning shore:
What else — I heed not — take from
me;
Leave but this glass of memory!

TIME'S SONG.

THE days come,
  And the days go!
The bees hum
  Where the roses blow:
The days go,
  And the leaves burn:
The birds know,
  And to home return.

The days come,
  And the days go!
And all dumb
  Lies the world in snow:
The days go,
  And the year's rhyme
Is made so
  By the poet, Time!

ATTAINMENT.

FROM the marble of his thought
Are the poet's fancies wrought
Into forms of symmetry,
Into rhyme and melody:
Not by any magic feat
Comes the statue forth complete;
Only patient labor, long,
Can create the perfect song;
Only love that does not tire
Can attain its high desire, —
Love that deems no gift of time
Wasted, so it win the rhyme
One elusive word to start
Life within the lyric's heart.
Still the Parthenon for us —
Jewel of Pentelicus
Fashioned centuries ago —
Shines with undiminished glow;
Still the resurrected bust,
Buried ages in the dust,
Holds to-day its honored place
By the marvel of its grace;

So the poet's song shall shine
For the jewel of one line;
So his lyric shall endure
Be the carven marble pure.
Toil he must if he would win
Heaven's gate and enter in;
Labor of a life-time give
That the sculptured verse shall live!

ALLAH'S HOUSE.

NÁNÁC, the faithful, pausing once to pray,
From holy Mecca turned his face away.

A Moslem priest, who chanced to see him there
Forgetful of the attitude in prayer,

Cried, "Infidel, how durst thou turn thy feet
Toward Allah's house — the sacred temple's seat?"

To whom the pious Nánác thus replied:
"Know'st thou God's house is, as the world is, wide?

"Thou, turn them if thou canst toward any spot
Where mighty Allah's awful house is not?"

PERPETUITY.

I HEARD a sweet voice singing in the night
A tender love-song written years ago,
To ease a poet's heart of that deep woe
Born of long absence from its dear delight;
And as the music like a bird took flight
Across the shadowed world and vanished so,
I thought of him who wrote it, — did he know
How Time would keep his jewel-lyric bright?

O Poet of to-day, whose heart would sing
Some simple song of love, and sweet words give
To mate the melody that thrills the lute, —

Sing on, nor heed what lips are murmuring
To scorn your art: one perfect song shall live
For love and you long after they are mute!

QUATRAINS.

I.

SUNRISE.

BLOOMS in the east when darkness goes
A radiant, cloud-petaled rose,
Out of whose iridescent heart
The yellow bees of sunlight dart.

II.

MOONRISE.

WITHIN this silent palace of the Night,
See how the moon, like some huge, phantom moth,
Creeps slowly up across the azure cloth
That hangs between the darkness and the light.

III.

A HOLLYHOCK.

SERAGLIO of the Sultan Bee!
I listen at the waxen door,

And hear the zithern's melody
  And sound of dancing on the floor.

IV.

WINTER'S BEGGAR.

Where heedless winds around him blow,
  The Tree, a tattered beggar, stands,
  And reaches out his empty hands
To catch the silver of the snow.

V.

CONTRAST.

In her dark hair a lustrous jewel gleams,
  A single star upon the edge of night:
Dazzling it is, and yet how dull it seems
  Beside her face, — drowned in the morning's light.

VI.

SUN AND MOON.

By day in Allah's azure urn
The sun, a fire, is made to burn:
And from its ashes there by night
The moon, a lily, blossoms white.

VII.

SURF MUSIC.

LYING beside the margin of the deep,
I hear the music of mysterious streams
Sung by the waves; — like voices heard in dreams
Moving along the shadowed shore of sleep.

VIII.

LYRICS.

IN Nature's open book
An epic is the sea,
A lyric is the brook: —
Lyrics for me!

LOVE

AN OLD SONG.

OFTENTIMES there come to me
Scraps of music-memory
That have slept, alas, how long!
In the quiet night of song.
I can mark the measured time,
I can catch the notes that rhyme,
Till it seems I almost hear
Whispered words within my ear;
Yet, for all I listen so
To them as they come and go,
Shreds of only one refrain
In my memory remain.

Long ago the song was sung,
Long ago, when I was young,
And my heart in time would beat
With the music soft and sweet.
There was something that would start
Glad emotions in my heart,
Something in the words which made
Joy grow bright and sorrow fade,

Something in the notes of joy
Giving courage to the boy
Long ago, ere he began
Dreaming of the present man.

Never comes this strain but I
Seem to feel her standing by.
Oh, that all the notes might come
Back from lips forever dumb,
So that I might render whole
This marred music of the soul!
Oh, that I again might bring
Back this song she used to sing!
I should sing it till my eyes,
Through a rift in Paradise,
Caught a vision of her face
Smiling from her dwelling-place;
I should sing it line by line
Till her lips should answer mine;
I should sing it o'er and o'er
Till I seemed a boy once more,—
Till my dream should bring in truth
Her who sang it to my youth!

THE LAST LETTER.

Long years within its sepulchre
  Of faintly scented cedar
Has lain this letter dear to her
  Who was its constant reader:
The postmark on the envelope
  Sufficed the date to give her,
And told the birth of patient hope
  That managed to outlive her.

How often to this treasure-box,
  Tears in her eyes' soft fringes,
She came with key and turned the locks,
  And on its brazen hinges
Swung back the quaintly figured lid,
  And raised a sandal cover,
Disclosing, under trinkets hid,
  This message from her lover.

Then lifting it as 't were a child,
  Her hand awhile caressed it
Ere to the lips that sadly smiled
  Time and again she pressed it:

Then drew the small inclosure out
  And smoothed the wrinkled paper,
Lest any line should leave a doubt
  Or any word escape her.

Still held the olden charm its place
  Amid the tender phrases;
Time seemed unwilling to efface
  The love-pervaded praises:
And though a thousand lovers might
  Have matched them all for passion,
A poet were inspired to write
  In their unstudied fashion.

From "Darling" slowly, word by word,
  She read the tear-stained treasure:
The mists by which her eyes were blurred
  Grew out of pain and pleasure;
But when she reached that cherished name,
  And saw the last leave-taking,
The mist a storm of grief became, —
  Her very heart was breaking!

I put it back, — this old-time note,
  Which seems like sorrow's leaven,
For she who read, and he who wrote,
  Please God, are now in heaven.

If lovers of to-day could win
  Such love as won this letter,
The world about us would begin
  To gladden and grow better.

PEPITA.

Up in her balcony where
  Vines through the lattices run
Spilling a scent on the air,
  Setting a screen to the sun,
Fair as the morning is fair,
    Sweet as a blossom is sweet,
    Dwells in her rosy retreat
        Pepita.

Often a glimpse of her face,
  When the wind rustles the vine
Parting the leaves for a space,
  Gladdens this window of mine;
Pink in its leafy embrace,
    Pink as the morning is pink,
    Sweet as a blossom I think
        Pepita.

I who dwell over the way
  Watch where Pepita is hid,
Safe from the glare of the day,
  Like an eye under its lid:

Over and over I say —
    Name like the song of a bird,
    Melody shut in a word, —
        " Pepita."

Look where the little leaves stir!
  Look, the green curtains are drawn!
There in a blossomy blur
  Breaks a diminutive dawn —
Dawn and the pink face of her!
    Name like a lisp of the south,
    Fit for a rose's small mouth, —
        Pepita!

HER SMILE HIS SUNLIGHT.

SWEETHEART, when rhymes I make
For your dear sake,
You bring
Into your face a smile
To cheer me while
I sing.

Like to that bird am I,
Which, when the sky
At night
A deeper azure grows,
No longer knows
Delight;

Or like of flowers that one
Which loves the sun,
And gives
The beauty of its bloom
To him for whom
It lives:

Pleasure nor joy to bless
Have I unless
Your face
Over my paper shines
And lights the lines
With grace.

For me your smile is day—
The golden ray
That climbs
Imagination's wall
And sweetens all
My rhymes.

For you the bird's song, this;
The flower's fresh kiss
And breath:
Nor may their nightfall come
Till both are dumb
In death!

TO A ROSE.

Go, Rose, and in her golden hair
  You shall forget the garden soon;
The sunshine is a captive there
  And crowns her with a constant noon.

And when your spicy odor goes,
  And fades the beauty of your bloom,
Think what a lovely hand, O Rose,
  Shall place your body in the tomb!

UNDER HER BALCONY.

Up, slender vine, your love is mine;
I watch you as you go,
A lyric budding line on line
With blossom-rhymes a-row!
Up, up, until her window-sill,
Like Heaven's gate in sight,
Makes all your heart with hope to fill
And bloom with its delight!

And when her eyes' soft twilight lies
Upon you nestled there,
When all about you is surprise,
And all below, despair,
Then to my Sweet, my love repeat;
Yield her one perfect bloom,
Which, though it perish at her feet,
May, ghostlike, haunt her room.

But if her mind and heart be kind,
And grant you gracious rest,
And for this gift a pillow find,
And fold it to her breast, —

Up, up! I burn my fate to learn
  From her who waits above;
Let but a leaf to earth return,—
  Her answer and her love!

AD ASTRA.

Blossom, little stars, and fill
  The garden of the sky;
Drops of wine that you distil
  Upon the grasses lie.

Every thirsty blade holds up
  A blessing to the blue,
Every thirsty flower its cup
  Fills with the heaven's dew.

Blossom, little stars of love,
  In my beloved's heart;
Blossom like the stars above,
  And into gladness start. .

Far beneath you there is one
  Who dares a cup to raise:
He has thirsted in the sun
  These many dreary days.

Blossom, blossom soon, and bring
  Love's gladness and the wine
To revive the hopes that spring
  Up in this heart of mine.

CONTENTMENT.

A GIRL to love, a pipe to smoke,
  Enough to eat and drink;
A friend with whom to crack a joke,
  And one to make me think;
A book or two of simple prose,
  A thousand more of rhyme:
No matter then how fast Time goes,
  I take no heed of Time!

The little wife inspires my thought
  With serious intent;
She cheers me with her wisdom fraught
  With love and sentiment:
Or prose to read, or rhyme to sing,
  She makes them each sublime:
No matter then how Time takes wing,
  I take no heed of Time!

God grant me that when grown so old
  Nor pipe nor glass I crave,
The little wife and books may hold
  My heart unto the grave:

There let me sleep in peace below
  The turf, where ivies climb:
No matter then how Time shall go,
  I take no heed of Time!

HELIOTROPE.

Go, Heliotrope,
  Unto my Sweet and tell
How, like a harbinger of hope,
  You come to dwell
    Near her, and pray to rest
    Upon her breast.

Tell her for me
  In whispers of perfume,
How like the golden sun is she,
  To which your bloom
    Forever turns its face
    Beseeching grace.

Say, even so
  The blossom of my love
Looks from its land of doubt below
  To her above,
    Waiting one word to slip
    Her scarlet lip.

Then if you feel
  Her heart with joy beat fast,
Or if with one sweet kiss she seal
  Your lips at last,
    And leave you stricken dumb
    Until I come:

Seeing you there
  Upon her bosom, I
Shall know what answer to my prayer
  She makes, and lie
    Beside you dumb with bliss,
    Sealed by her kiss.

VALENTINES.

I.

LOVE, at your door young Cupid stands
  And knocks for you to come:
The frost is in his feet and hands,
  His lips with cold are numb.
Grant him admittance, sweetheart mine,
  And by your cheering fire
His lips shall loosen as with wine
  And speak forth my desire.

He left me not an hour ago,
  And when the rascal went
Barefooted out into the snow,
  I asked him whither bent.
Quoth he: "To her whose face is like
  A garden full of flowers:
To her whose smiles like sunlight strike
  Across the winter hours."

No more he said, nor need of more
  Had I to know. I knew
His path lay straight unto your door:
  That face belongs to you!

"Godspeed," I cried, "and give her this,
  When you her face shall see;"
And on his lips I set a kiss,
  A valentine from me!

II.

I CARE not that the snow lies deep
  Upon the world about:
The hidden flowers, they lie asleep
  And dream, and never doubt
But Spring shall come again and set
  The rubies on the vine:
The faithful Year shall not forget
        Her valentine.

I care not that a thousand miles
  Keep me and mine apart,
For when upon this page she smiles
  And gladdens in her heart,
Like Spring, the sun returns to me
  And cheers these eyes of mine:
My sweetheart promises to be
        My valentine.

Be still, my heart, and like the flowers
  Asleep beneath the snow,
Dream on, and soon the sunny hours
  Shall wake you dreaming so:

And when the Summer's stars above
Drip with their dewy wine,
The flowers shall come, and with them, love,
And valentine!

ON A CLOCK.

LONELY once, my love away,
  To this slave of Time I cried:
  " Faster on your journey glide,
Let your feet no second stay;
Speed the dreary night and day!"
    He, all heedless, obstinate,
    Never quickened in his gait.

Happy once, my love in sight,
  To this slave of Time I prayed:
  " Be your journey slowly made,
Loiter with me in delight;
Stay the happy day and night!"
    Obstinate, he heard at last,—
    Heard, and hurried twice as fast.

TO WINTER.

Good Winter, hear this wish I write
 Before the red leaves blow
  Across the sky
  To droop and die,
 And sleep beneath the snow;
Before the birds have taken flight
 Unto a gentler clime,
  And for my thought
  Have left me naught
 Of melody or rhyme.

The purple clusters in the leaves
 Of grapes already ripe;
  The chestnut burrs
  Half burst; the slurs
 Upon the robin's pipe;
The shrill wind whistling round the eaves;
 The dawn's white gossamer;—
  All these awake
  The wish I make,
 Good Winter, just for her.

My Love, a blossom fair is she;
  Lithe as a lily stem:
    Her voice and words
    So like the birds'
  Will make you think of them.
Good Winter, keep her safe for me,
  Leave to her face its smile,
    And to her heart
    Of love that part
  Which makes my wish worth while!

HIS STARLIGHT.

You who at my elbow sit,
By whose eyes my lines are lit,
How shall any poet's pen
Go amiss or falter when
Stars like these shine out above —
Beacons kindled there by Love —
Lighting up the paths below
Where he wanders to and fro.

Is it strange the rhymes should kiss
Under such a spell as this?
They but mimic those, my Sweet,
Who of old were wont to meet,
Meet and linger at the bars,
Making love beneath the stars:
We ourselves were happy rhymes
In those dear, betrothal times.

Take this lyric: every line
But reflects the stars that shine
O'er my shoulder, telling me
Of my sweetheart's constancy!

And if any word appear
Vague or needless, say you: *Here*
Went a cloud across his skies;
This is where its shadow lies.

But should any turn of phrase
Win your lips to speak its praise,
Know you then the happy thought
From your eyes the poet caught:
All the graces of his song
To those constant stars belong,—
To those tender eyes that brim
Full with love to gladden him.

UNSPOKEN.

LOVE, when we parted, you and I,
  Who had been friends so many years,
How many times a last good-by
  Rose to the surface of my tears!

There never once to it you cast
  A strand of hope its life to save,
But watched it to the very last,
  And saw it sink into its grave.

And now to you, away so far,
  The winging of that spirit-word
As futile seems as to a star
  The flight of some enamored bird!

SONG.

SONG like a rose should be;
  Each rhyme a petal sweet;
For fragrance, melody,
  That when her lips repeat
    The words, her heart may know
    What secret makes them so:—
        Love, only Love!

Go, then, my song,—a rose
  Fashioned of love and rhyme;
Unto her heart disclose
  That secret old as time,—
    Old, yet forever new!
    Go, then, and tell her true:—
        Love, only Love!

THE NUN'S ROSE.

OVER the convent wall
  Clambers a rose-vine sweet,
Letting its fragrant blossoms fall
  Into the dusty street.

Hither the weary guest,
  Drawn by the fresh perfume,
Pauses to dream awhile and rest
  Under the spray of bloom:

Lingers to dream of those
  Who, in their quiet hours,
Dwelling within the garden-close,
  Wander among the flowers.

What of their holy deeds
  Ponders the dreamer there?
Is it the rosaries of beads
  Counted in silent prayer?

Is it the chants they sing?
  Is it the fasts they keep?

Is it the words of comforting
  Spoken to those who weep?

Nay, 't is of her whose love
  Moved her to train this vine
Over the convent wall above,
  Breathing a scent like wine.

Tokens these blossoms seem
  Speaking of her pure life:
Petals that fall like dream on dream
  Into a world of strife.

MEMORIES.

LONG time she sat, yet never touched a string, —
Her thoughts were all of one far, far away,
One dearly loved, whose face to her could bring
Desire to play.

The tune — ah, well she knew it! — and the words
So full of tenderness, unsung so long,
Hung on her parted lips — a flock of birds
Without a song.

Anon, the music to her finger-tips
In swift pulsations from her glad heart went,
Then quavered to the song upon her lips
The instrument.

For suddenly across the strings she swept
Her slender hand, and lo, there came at last
The melody which had in silence slept
The whole year past.

Faintly at first, with every touch it grew
More sweet, and filled the charmèd air around,
And sang within her ears until she knew
'T was joy she found.

And there, alone, she held the graceful form
And sang to it as 't were a babe at rest,
Singing itself to sleep and growing warm
Against her breast.

So, happy in the melody she wrought
Upon the old guitar in her embrace,
Her eyes grew heavy, closed, and slumber brought
Dreams of his face.

DIRGE.

LET a song be softly sung;
  Let a prayer be said;
Let a solemn bell be rung;—
      Love is dead!

With the early buds he came,
  When the snows were fled;
Lightly lisped the leaves his name
      Overhead:

Sang the birds a sweeter strain;
  Troops of roses red
Followed in a laughing train
      Where he led:

Brighter beamed the stars above,
  And the soft gales sped
Whispering the secret: *Love*
      Soon shall wed!

Rang the bells in merry chime
  When the promise spread:
Poets strung with beads of rhyme
      Fancy's thread.

Fragrant petals lightly fell
  Where his feet might tread:
Blossoms that he loved so well
    Were his bed.

There he slumbers, pale and cold:
  Let a tear be shed;
Let a solemn bell be tolled; —
    Love is dead!

NOCTURNE.

Love, throw thy lattice open to the night,
And shame the moon, that doth so sadly shine
Upon the world, with that glad face of thine!
Look down upon me with thine eyes more bright
Than those of angels from yon dizzy height
Of heaven peering out; and be it mine
To feel uplifted to thee, like a vine
Led up the trellis ladder by the light!

Then, while the earth in purple shadows deep
Lies hushed, and, dreaming, slumber all the birds,
And not a whisper wakes the leaves above, —

Listen, and thou shalt hear the lute-strings weep
In music soft, mourning to win thy words
To make complete their melody of love!

REMEMBRANCE.

DAY to my heart
With you comes always fair:
When you depart
'T is twilight there.

Then love unbars
The door of dreams for me,
And lights the stars
Of memory.

NATURE

A GREETING FOR SPRING.

LET us go forth and meet her
  As she comes through the eastern gates;
Let us away to greet her
  Whom the lover-like land awaits
In a rapturous mood to bless,
All impatient for her caress;
Let us mount up the purple slopes
That are murmurous with their hopes;
And the winds speeding on before
  In their haste to be first shall sing
Of the earth's wide floor,
That is dotted o'er
  With the emerald steps of Spring.

Moses upon the mountains
  Strikes his rod on the marble snow,
Freeing the crystal fountains;
  And the streams through the plains below
Are her couriers swift, who run
In the glow of the golden sun

Through the fields on their twinkling feet,
With the gladdening promise sweet, —
She is coming with laughing eyes
From the Orient's sun-wrapped land,
From the land that lies
Under tranquil skies
Like an opal in Allah's hand.

Up at the dawn's first waking
From her dreams in the night's long gloom!
Up when the east is breaking
Like a rose into scarlet bloom!
When the buds in the branches shine,
And the blood of the slender vine
From the tip of each tiny stem
Oozes out and becomes a gem,
Till the world like a queen is drest
For a carnival glad and gay,
And awaits her guest
In the curtained west
At the odorous doors of day.

Hark! on the breeze a rally
And a rustle of wings is heard!
Over the misty valley
Soars a heavenly singing bird
Like a sapphire that burns with song;

And it drops to the earth erelong,
Where it kindles a mighty choir
Into flames of a lyric fire;
And the jewel that falls to earth
  In the silvery sod is set,
And it marks the birth
Out of winter's dearth
  Of a delicate violet.

Let us go forth and linger
  At the gates with the sunrise bars;
Watch for her rosy finger
  As she slips off its ring of stars,
And her radiant face which gleams
With the joy of the year's sweet dreams,
And her eyes like the morning dews,
And her cheeks with the wild-flower
    hues;
Let us watch till the east grows bright
  With her glorious robe that falls
Like a wave of light
On the shore of night,
  And the bird to the valley calls.

Oh, for the fragrant presage
  Of the goddess divinely fair!
Oh, for the flute-like message,
  Making melody float mid-air!

For the flash of the blue-bird's wings!
For the gush of the woodland springs!
For the buds in the vine-clad bowers,
And the breath of the gentle flowers!
We shall know them at morning, when
  All the shadows of night are furled;
We shall know them then,—
It is Spring again,
  And her smile is upon the world!

NOONTIDE.

No leaf is stirring in the tree,
  The drowsy bird forgets his tune;
The flower, forsaken by the bee,
  Hangs silent in the glaring noon.

Hushed is the murmur of the stream
  Whose music made the morning sweet,
And on its tranquil bosom dream
  The languid lilies in the heat.

And in these cradles gently rocked
  When idle eddies catch the stems,
Their gauzy wings in slumber locked,
  Repose the dragon-flies like gems.

This is the golden hour of rest,
  When, half his circling journey done,
Midway between the east and west
  The zenith holds the eager sun.

And not until his fetters break
  And fall in shadows on the ground,
Shall any slumberer awake,
  Or Nature know a breath or sound.

THE SKY-SHIP.

In the soft wind that blows,
  Yon cloud-ship of the sky
Spreads a white sail and throws
  A shadow where I lie.

And with my dream is blent
  A breath of spice and gums
Out of the Orient,
  Betraying whence she comes.

Unto a land remote
  To fill its rich bazaars
Sails this Arabian boat
  Amid the island stars,

And in yon harbor calm
  Of Heaven's ocean blue,
Empties her freight of balm
  The twilight's fragrant dew!

A WOODLAND SPRING.

BENEATH the trees whose lisping brood
  With every breath of summer wake,
And in the grove's green solitude
  Soft music make,

A sylvan deity her pool
  Of crystal water deep has hid,
Perpetually fresh and cool,
  The rocks amid.

Gray, like a carpet, lies the moss,
  To shield from ragged stones her feet;
And for a roof the branches cross
  Above and meet.

Birds in these rafters build and mate,
  And rear their lyric-hearted throng,
And teach them well to imitate
  Her happy song.

Hither came I upon a time
  To rest me in the tranquil shade,

Led by a brook whose limpid rhyme
  Its source betrayed.

I watched these minstrels, pair by pair,
  Come to the fountain's pebbly brink
And, pausing first as if in prayer,
  Dip down and drink.

They seemed to know the goddess who
  Presided o'er this woodland spring;
And I, who longed to know her too,
  Bade them to sing.

Then, as they sang, awhile I knelt
  In worship at her sylvan shrine;
And even as I prayed I felt
  Her lips touch mine!

THE NAIAD'S CUP.

THIS is a naiad's drinking cup
The water's tireless arm held up;
In it no drops of wine remain,
Its chaste lip wears no crimson stain.

No footprint by the water's edge
Betrays to whom she drank the pledge;
Only this empty cup whose lip
Speaks naught of its companionship.

Who knows but for this chalice white
A star was stolen from the night,
From whose clear jewel-grape was drawn
The dew of some Parnassian dawn;

And as the precious wine distilled,
One drop into the water spilled,
Pervading all the purple deep
Wherein this naiad lay asleep!

Such potency that flavor knew,
Her dream told where this lily grew;

One taste, and she awoke, and then
Her eyes saw Arcady again!

The East was reddening; the West
Was shepherding the stars to rest;
But ere Apollo's reign began
She pledged this loving cup with Pan!

ETERNITY LANE.

THE fence on either side is down,
  Or buried under vines and bushes,
Save where, determined not to drown,
  A picket through the tangle pushes.

On its gray peak the birds alight
  And trill their carols brief and tender;
All day a beacon, golden bright,
  It shines in solitary splendor.

But through the creepers' leafy wall
  No gleam of sunlight ever passes
To break the night that shadows all
  The cobwebbed growth of groping
    grasses.

The rain that rattles on the leaves
  Outside with such a happy laughter,
Once captive in this prison, grieves
  For light and liberty long after.

No traveler for years has set
  His foot upon the pathway hidden;
Nor through the weeds forever wet
  For years has any horseman ridden.

No rut remains of wagon-road;
  The gateway has no gate to span it;
Only the bat and bulging toad
  Dare venture past the posts of granite.

One dreams, so silent is the place
  With all its life and light departed,
That Time has finished here the race,
  And now Eternity has started!

STORM.

THE sun sank red in the dull gray west
Like a glowing coal in a bed of ashes;
The river writhed in a mad unrest
As it felt the scourge of the wind's keen lashes;
No star outshone on the Night's dark breast
Scarred with livid lines of the lightning's flashes:
And he came with a voice of thunder
O'er the mountains that trembled under,
And a sudden thrill
Ran from hill to hill,
And the valley was dumb with wonder.

Then all night long on the tangled strings
Of the tempest's lute did the wind awaken
Discordant notes from their slumberings,
And the forest cried like a soul forsaken.

The storm-bird fluttered his dismal wings
And the rain-wrapt land like a leaf was shaken!
And he called in a voice of thunder
O'er the mountains that rumbled under,
And the hosts of flame
From the heavens came,
And the valley was filled with wonder.

But lo, dawn smiles, and the misty world
Like a pearl is plucked from its ocean dreaming;
The storm's dark pinions at last are furled
In the fragrant hush of the sun's bright gleaming,
And where the arrows of fire were hurled,
Lo, the face of Heaven with gladness beaming!
God has silenced the voice of thunder
O'er the mountains that echoed under,
And the bird's sweet song
In the air grows strong,
And the valley is hushed with wonder!

IN THE CLOVER.

In the pasture's clover deep
There I love to lie and sleep,
Over me the placid sky,
Blue save where his golden eye
Out of Heaven's window looks
In the mirrors of the brooks,
That Apollo may behold
How like me he too grows old;
All about me billows blown,
Emerald as Ocean's own,
By the drowsy gales that blow,
Catching fragrance as they go.

Crusoe of that clover isle,
There I come to dream awhile,
Far from worry, strife, or din,
Shut my island home within.
Deep-drawn breaths of winy air
Are the nectar I drink there;
Hebe ne'er her draughts served up
Brimming such a sapphire cup!
Thessaly ne'er grew a vine
Yielding such a sparkling wine,

Drinking which 't is mine to feel
Blissful languor o'er me steal!

Give me then that clover bed
With its blue roof overhead,
There to lie and dream away
All the tedious hours of day.
Pan shall cheer me with his reed,
Fauns shall dance across the mead,
Daphnis tend his snowy herds,
And Theocritus make words
Mingle in soft melody
In my slumber-Sicily
Set the clover sea amid,
As in olden days he did!

WINTER STARLIGHT.

THE air is keen, the sky is clear;
The wind has gone in whispers down;
And, gleaming in the atmosphere,
A jewel, lies the lighted town.

The winter's mantle stretches white
Upon the roofs and streets below;
All hushed the noises of the night
Against the bosom of the snow.

The Moon from her blue dwelling-place
Smiles over all, so pale, so fair,
It seems the Earth's wan, winter face
Reflected in a mirror there.

Far off the lonely trees uplift
Their naked branches like the spars
Of some deserted ship adrift
Under a canopy of stars.

It is the darkened world that rides
The sea of space, forever drawn
By secret winds and mighty tides
Unto the harbor of the Dawn!

DAYBREAK.

UNTO his parching lips a cup
Brimming with wine the hills hold up,
Fresh with the breath of bud and bloom,
Cooled in the caves of purple gloom.
One long, deep draught he takes, and
then
Into his saddle leaps again,
Scatters the gold coins left and right,
And speeds beyond the gates of night:
The Years are at his heels, — away!
The Sun still leads them by a day.

BOOKS

ASPIRATION.

WITHIN the meadow of Time's book
Let my song be the laughing brook
That sings along its silver way
As 't were a dryad gone astray,
Seeking by music's balm to bless
The hunger of its loneliness.
Let all my lines like ripples run
Forever mirroring the sun;
Gay as the light lisp of a leaf,
Unmarred by any gust of grief;
Sweet as the soft south wind that blows
Its tender love-song to the rose.
So, later, if my rhymes be read
By maid or youth, it may be said:
No melancholy strain he knew;
His skies were always bright and blue.
Life seemed for him to slip along
As smoothly as his limpid song,
Which, in its grace and simple art,
Echoes the gladness in his heart.

THE FLY-LEAF TO THE READER.

FRIEND, stay your steps awhile before
You pass within the open door;
Bethink you in what manner you
Shall greet the host; consider, too,
How to a feast of all his best
The author here invites his guest,
To taste his meat and drink his wine,
On every dish to freely dine.
And, mind you, when you come to sit
Before the board whereon his wit
And wisdom are all spread to make
A meal for your mind's stomach's sake,
To bear yourself with dignity
And treat your host with courtesy.

If any dish before you placed
By any chance offend your taste,
Or if the food seem wanting aught
Of proper seasoning, say naught.
Eat quietly, and when you go
Forget not gratitude to show;

And, being gone, if you repent
The precious time that you have spent,
Or think that you have poorly fared
Upon the food and drink prepared,
Curse not this book — the wine and meat
So kindly offered you to eat.
The author, too, spare from your curse,
And do not go from bad to worse;
You were his guest, this recollect,
And treat him only with respect.
Keep your opinions to yourself,
And put the book back on the shelf.
Think this: what one may eat, and die,
Another's taste may satisfy.

THE LIBRARY.

GIVE me the room whose every nook
Is dedicated to a book:
Two windows will suffice for air
And grant the light admission there;
One looking to the south, and one
To speed the red, departing sun.
The eastern wall from frieze to plinth
Shall be the Poet's labyrinth,
Where one may find the lords of rhyme
From Homer's down to Dobson's time:
And at the northern side a space
Shall show an open chimney-place,
Set round with ancient tiles that tell
Some legend old, and weave a spell
About the firedog-guarded seat,
Where, musing, one may taste the heat:
Above, the mantel should not lack
For curios and bric-à-brac, —
Not much, but just enough to light
The room up when the fire is bright.
The volumes on this wall should be
All prose and all philosophy,

From Plato down to those who are
The dim reflections of that star;
And these tomes all should serve to show
How much we write — how little know;
For since the problem first was set
No one has ever solved it yet.
Upon the shelves along the west
The scientific books shall rest;
Beside them, History; above, —
Religion, — hope, and faith, and love:
Lastly, the southern wall should hold
The story-tellers, new and old;
Haroun al Raschid, who was truth
And happiness to all my youth,
Shall have the honored place of all
That dwell upon the sunny wall;
And with him there shall stand a throng
Of those who help mankind along
More by their fascinating lies
Than all the learning of the wise.

Such be the library; and take
This motto of a Latin make
To grace the door through which I pass:
Hic habitat Felicitas!

FORGOTTEN BOOKS.

OF books I sing, but not of those
Which any book collector knows, —
The priceless, rare editions, not, —
But volumes which the World forgot
And with them those who wrote, as well,
Before they had a chance to sell:
Ephemerals that find themselves
With the Immortals on my shelves.
I name no names, for if I should
None would recall them now, nor could
A word of mine bring any one
Out of its long Oblivion.
The ink on many fly-leaves still
Looks quite as fresh as when the quill
On each inscribed an author's name,
And signed his title there to Fame
Without one solitary fear
About its being proven clear.

One has its pages still uncut,
Clean, kept ironically shut
By him whose name therein is penned
Above: *From his devoted friend.*

But not infrequently I come
Across the imprint of a thumb,
Or in the paragraphs I find
A pleasing sentence underlined,
Or neatly on the margin set
A compliment in epithet:
Each one of these, I 'm satisfied,
Was read before its author died.

And there is one among them all,
Morocco bound, gilt-edged, and small,
Filled with the amatory rhymes
Of ante-Tennysonian times,
Stiff in their phraseology
And rather rough in melody.
'T is *Dedicated unto Her*
By Her Unworthy Worshipper.
And just below is written, "*These*
Many and pleasing Melodies,
Dear Wm. writ in '98,
& unto Me did Dedicate."
This one was read and read again,
And annotated by her pen:
And this fulfilled the Author's hopes,
Repaid the toil of all his tropes,
And had, at least his span of life,
One constant reader in his wife.

TO HIS BOOK.

Go, little book with heart of rhyme,
This is our last leave-taking time:
For you the journey stretches long,
With naught to cheer you save a song;
For me, alas! when you depart,
A doubtful, desolated heart.
I have but slender hope to give
To gladden such a fugitive.
The world may greet you well or ill,
Seeing your way lies all up hill:
But o'er that summit dim and far
I catch a glimpse of one sure star
Which shines to guide you and to bring
You ever closer there to sing.
Little I care for praise or blame
Unless it whispers of her name:
Her praise is inspiration's breath;
Her scorn were aspiration's death!
Go, then, and if she welcome you
I care not what the world may do!

www.ingramcontent.com/pod-product-compliance
Lightning Source LLC
LaVergne TN
LVHW021427110826
845150LV00007B/2120

9781425507121